# CRACK

The temptation to try crack and other drugs may confront students in all kinds of schools.

THE DRUG ABUSE PREVENTION LIBRARY

# CRACK

Rodney G. Peck

THE ROSEN PUBLISHING GROUP, INC.
NEW YORK

*The people pictured in this book are only models. They in no way practice or endorse the activities illustrated. Captions serve only to explain the subjects of photographs and do not in any way imply a connection between the real-life models and the staged situations.*

Published in 1991, 1993, 1997 by the Rosen Publishing Group, Inc.
29 East 21st Street, New York, NY 10010

**Revised Edition 1997**

Manufactured in the United States of America

**Library of Congress Cataloging-in-Publication Data**

Peck, Rodney G.
  Crack / Rodney G. Peck
  (The drug abuse prevention library)
  Includes bibliographical references and index.
  Summary: Discusses the characteristics of crack cocaine and the
    dangers of using the drug.
  ISBN 0-8239-2618-4
  1. Crack (Drug)—Juvenile literature. 2. Cocaine habit—Juvenile
    literature. [1. Crack (Drug). 2. Cocaine habit. 3. Drug abuse.]
    I. Title. II. Series.
  HV5809.5.P43 1991
  362.29'8—dc20                               91-11141
                                                CIP
                                                AC

# Contents

Teenagers sometimes try drugs just because they are forbidden.

# CHAPTER 1

# The Road to Drug Dependence

In 1991, the movie *New Jack City* starring Wesley Snipes, Ice-T, and Chris Roc portrayed the effects of crack to mainstream America. Many filmgoers were shocked by the scenes of drug use in the movie. Ruthless drug dealers got young people hooked on crack by selling it to them cheaply at first, then demanding more money. The users were too addicted to the powerful drug to resist. Needing money to buy more crack, they turned to crime. They stole and even killed to get the money to buy more crack.

Meanwhile, in cities where crack was sold, crime rose dramatically. Addicts suffered terrible health problems, and many died. Hospital wards were burdened by

**8** sick addicts and by "crack babies" who were born sick because their mothers smoked the drug during pregnancy.

Crack had slowly been invading larger cities in the United States throughout the 1980s, but this popular film made people wake up to the drug's dangers. In the 1990s, it became apparent that crack is not just an inner-city problem. Cheap and easy to make, crack is available all over the country. Many young people are trying it. One recent study reported record use of cocaine among students in grades 6–12.

Like many young people, Sara experimented with drugs. When Sara started using marijuana, she would smoke one joint (marijuana cigarette) to get high. After a few months of regular use, Sara's body had changed a lot. It became used to one joint. Then she had to smoke two joints to reach the high that she used to get with only one.

Sara's friend Paul didn't smoke pot. He drank beer. When he first started drinking, two beers made him drunk. But after only a few months of drinking, his body changed, too. It got used to those two cans of beer. Now Paul needs three or four cans of beer to get drunk.

This change in the body is called *toler-ance*. Sara's body built up a tolerance to marijuana. Paul's body built up a toler-ance to alcohol. When the body builds tolerance, it needs more and more of a drug to reach the same high as before. The body will build tolerance to any drug, including alcohol, marijuana, tobacco, and crack.

In getting hooked, the next step is easy for Sara to fall into. She's already using drugs regularly. Her body has built up a tolerance to them. She then starts using drugs to celebrate, to relax, to feel at ease around other people, and for many other reasons. She now needs the drug to get through the week. She depends on the drug. That need for the drug is called *chemical dependency*. Drugs are chemicals that change the way your body works. Eventually your body can't function nor-mally without them.

When you are dependent on a drug, your body and mind need the drug. You don't have control over your use of the drug. Drug-dependent people suffer from *withdrawal* when they try to stop using. Withdrawal is the way the body reacts when it doesn't have the drug. Crack users

**10** suffer from withdrawal. Some crack users can't sleep. Sometimes they have hallucinations, or have trouble breathing.

Drug *addiction* is the last step for people like Sara and Paul. The drug use turns into a disease. Addicted people live for their drug. They think of almost nothing but their next high. They plan how much of the drug they'll buy and where they will get it. Drug addicts are hooked on the drug. They live to get high and depend on the drug to get them there.

Drug addicts have no control over their drug use. They can be addicted to more than one drug at a time. And addicts use drugs despite any bad effects the drugs might have, including death.

Drug dependence and addiction can happen to anyone. Rich people and poor people become addicts. People who live in the city, the suburbs, and in rural communities can become drug-dependent. It happens to people of all races. But some people, like Julian, are more vulnerable to drug addiction. They may become dependent on drugs more easily than others.

Julian's father uses cocaine. His older brother is addicted to crack. Julian has to be careful. He is in great danger of developing a drug addiction. Why? Studies show that the family members of drug addicts are more likely to become addicts than people without drug addicts in the family. Julian has the disease of drug addiction in his family. The disease can be passed from one generation to another. Julian is aware of the danger and he chooses not to use *any* drugs. He knows that any experimenting puts him at risk.

Crack is a dangerous drug. In this book you will learn why. You will read about how crack is made, and what it can do to your body. You will learn about how crack hurts everybody, not just users, by contributing to increases in crime. You will also learn how young people often start using crack after experimenting with drugs they think are less harmful, such as alcohol and tobacco. You will find out ways to avoid starting down the road to drug dependence. You will also find a list of organizations that can help you if you or a friend has a drug problem.

Even legal drugs become addictive. Some teenagers get hooked on cigarettes.

# CHAPTER 2

# Where Drug Problems Begin

*I*n most states, it is against the law for a person under twenty-one years of age to drink alcohol. It is also against the law for a person under eighteen to buy cigarettes. Many teenagers choose to ignore the laws. That is when drug use starts for many people. It starts when they are teenagers. And it usually starts with drugs such as tobacco and alcohol. Some teenagers also start with marijuana. That drug isn't legal for anyone.

Because alcohol and tobacco are legal, they are easy to get. In one survey, 80 percent of teenagers said that marijuana was also easy to get. Young people get these drugs from older brothers and sisters.

**14**    They get them from friends. They also get them from their parent's liquor cabinet or private stash.

The big question is: "Why do young people take drugs?" This is what some young people say:

### "I just want to forget my problems."

Danielle got drunk for the first time because she wanted to forget about a fight she had with her boyfriend. She took her parents' car and got into an accident. Getting drunk caused her more problems in the end.

### "I want to be cool."

There is nothing cool about damaging your brain or being so wasted that you can't remember where you've been or what you've done. Take a closer look at people who use crack. There is nothing cool about lying and stealing to buy another hit.

### "My older sister and her friends do it."

Watson felt like everyone treated him like a child. He wanted to look and act mature like his older sister Mai. One night during a party when a friend of his sister's offered him a crack pipe, he tried it. His heart pounded so hard he felt sick and had to leave the party.

### *"I'm sick of my parents telling me what to do."*

Using drugs to rebel can hurt your parents a great deal. But remember, it also hurts the people who take the drug. And sometimes it can even kill them. Taking drugs to rebel or to show anger hurts everybody and adds to your stress.

### *"My friends are using it."*

Sometimes it's really hard to say no to a friend. But a true friend won't force you to do something you don't want to do. People can be either leaders or followers. You can be a leader instead of agreeing to go along with something that could get all of you in trouble. Suggest fun things to do. You don't have to do anything just because your friends do it.

### *"I like the feeling of getting high."*

What kinds of things do you like to do? Seeing a funny movie can give you a good feeling. Spending time with friends or playing sports can give you good feelings. Many things in life make you feel good. Try concentrating on those things instead

**16** of risking your health and your future by using drugs.

### *"I want to be popular."*

Derek and Juan both were popular. Juan used drugs, but Derek didn't. One day Juan got caught with cocaine in his locker. He was suspended from school and taken to juvenile court. The story was on the local news. Now, he's well-known for being a drug user, not for being a good person. Derek is popular for being good at sports, and for being nice and funny. His popularity is based on qualities that will last.

### *"I was curious about drugs."*

Why be curious? You know that drugs can hurt or kill you. You wouldn't stand in front of a train to see how it would feel if it hit you. You know what would happen. Fast-moving trains and drugs are both dangerous. Both can kill you. It doesn't make sense to play with either one.

### *"It can't happen to me."*

Wrong! Almost every day we hear about people who have lost their jobs, their families, or their future because of drug use. Kids are kicked out of school for

Smoking and drinking are part of the party scene.

*18* using, possessing, or selling drugs. People die. It happens to others. But it can happen to you if you choose to use drugs.

Ask any addict if he or she is happy to be an addict. Nobody takes drugs wanting to become addicted. Everyone who is an addict once thought, "It can't happen to me." And now their lives are a mess.

Young people take drugs for many different reasons. But there are no good reasons. And there are no good drugs.

## *Gateway Drugs and Growing Bodies*

Even the drugs alcohol and tobacco that are legal for adults are very dangerous for growing teenagers. From the time you are born, your body starts growing. Your body keeps growing until you are between the ages of 19 and 22. During this time, it is important to give your body only good things. It doesn't take as much marijuana, alcohol, and tobacco as you may think to hurt a growing body.

The damage starts when a young person begins experimenting with drugs. Marijuana, alcohol, and tobacco are called "gateway drugs." They open the gate to harder drugs. Here is an example: A young body builds tolerance to alcohol. It takes more and more alcohol to get drunk. After a while, getting drunk takes too long. It becomes quicker and easier to smoke marijuana to get high. Then the body builds a tolerance to marijuana. The person looks for a quicker, stronger drug. The person moves on to cocaine or crack. Using tobacco, alcohol, or marijuana leads to using harder drugs. That's why they are called "gateway drugs."

A growing body can become addicted to a drug 10 times faster than an adult body. So a little experiment with drugs often leads to regular use of a drug.

The body is still changing during the teen years. It builds a tolerance to a drug very fast. Then, as you know, it takes more of the drug to reach the same high. Next, the young body starts to need the drug.

After using drugs, the young body has a damaged heart. The body has a changed brain. It has problems with its lungs, its eyes, and its muscles. The body may also have big problems with its *reproductive system*. That means that using drugs during the growing years may damage the ability to have children. This is another reason that taking drugs during the growing years is dangerous. By the time you

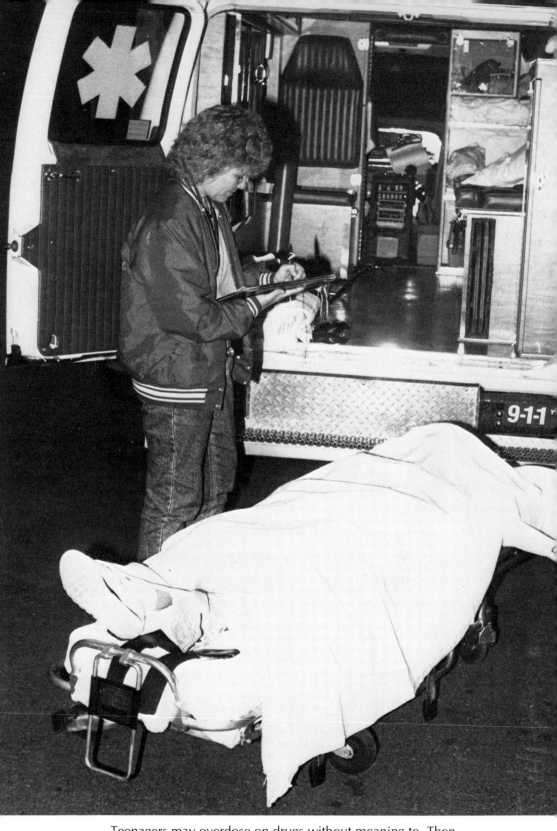

Teenagers may overdose on drugs without meaning to. Then they become accident statistics.

stop growing, your body may be in bad shape. Then you have to spend the rest of your life with a damaged body.

## *Choose the Road to a Bright Future*

Many young people get started on the road to drug dependence when they're teenagers. They may try alcohol or cigarettes in order to look cool or fit in. They may even try harder drugs like crack because they're curious or because they think everybody's doing it. These first steps can lead them toward addiction. Drug addicts suffer physical and mental health problems and usually end up getting in trouble with their families and the law.

You can choose to take the better road. Avoid alcohol and tobacco, which can lead to trying harder drugs later. Say no to people who pressure you to try drugs. Spend your time with friends who agree that drugs are harmful. Together, you can find fun, cool things to do that won't mess up your life in the end.

A drug habit leads the addict to crime to get money for more crack or cocaine.

# CHAPTER 3

# Cocaine

We've learned that tobacco, marijuana, and alcohol are gateway drugs. They open the gate to harder drugs. Cocaine is one of those harder drugs.

What is cocaine? Where does it come from? Why do people take cocaine? Here are some answers.

Cocaine is a very powerful stimulant. A stimulant makes your body work faster. It gives your body false energy. It speeds up your brain and your heart.

There are many names for cocaine. People call it "coke," "blow," or "snow." It is a white powder that people snort up the

**24** nose to get high. Some people inject cocaine or smoke cocaine. Any way you take it, it is a very dangerous drug.

Cocaine messes with your *central nervous system*. This system includes your brain and spinal cord. The central nervous system controls your entire body. When cocaine mixes up your central nervous system, your body doesn't know how to operate properly.

Where does cocaine come from? It comes from the *coca plant*. (Don't be confused. The coca plant is different from the *cacao plant*. The cacao plant gives us cocoa and chocolate.) The leaves of the coca plant contain a very small amount of cocaine.

The coca plant grows in the Andes Mountains of South America. The countries of Peru and Bolivia grow a lot of coca. The Inca Indians farm coca in the mountains. They pick the coca leaves to sell them.

It takes long hours and hard work to pick the leaves. The Indians chew the coca leaves to get the small amount of the drug they contain. It helps them stay awake and work more. Chewing the coca leaves is also part of their religion. However, most Incas live only to the age of thirty.

The Indians sell the coca leaves to drug dealers. The drug dealers turn the leaves into the white powder called cocaine. But how do they get cocaine from the coca leaves? Let's find out.

The cocaine is taken out of the coca leaves by mixing *kerosene* or *acid* with them. The mixing of coca leaves and acid is called *purifying*. So, when you take cocaine you are taking more than just cocaine powder.

Cocaine is taken from the coca leaves in two steps. First, the coca leaves are put in a press or steel drum with acid and crushed into a mash called "pasta." Then the pasta is mixed with another acid. The product is the white powder called cocaine. A person who snorts it is also snorting acid.

Hold on, our story is far from over. Other things besides acid are added to the cocaine that is sold on the street. Drug dealers add sugar, heroin, baby powder or other drugs to the powder. Here is an example: A drug dealer has one pound of cocaine. He mixes in a pound of sugar and heroin. Now he has two pounds of cocaine to sell. He will make much more money. The buyer never knows what he's getting. The buyer is even more at risk.

26    Cocaine is not a new drug in the United States. It was discovered more than 100 years ago. Scientists were searching for new medicines. They learned that the Incas chewed the leaves for energy. They also found that purifying the coca leaves gave them the strong drug called cocaine. Scientists thought that it was a safe cure for some illnesses. But many people became addicted to cocaine and many more died from it.

People decided that cocaine was not harmless. In 1906 a law was passed that limited the use of cocaine in medicines. However, cocaine can be used as a pain-killer (anesthetic) in certain operations on the nose and throat. It makes the skin numb. Only special doctors are allowed to use cocaine in very small amounts for operations.

Cocaine is a strong and dangerous drug. People can become dependent on it after one-time use. The drug dealer knows this fact. A drug-dependent person will usually do anything and pay any price to get the high. A dealer may charge a user anywhere from $45 to $100 for a single gram of cocaine. Often the dealer will give cocaine to teens for free at first.

Cocaine is expensive: A few hits cost a lot of dollars.

If a kid takes it and becomes addicted, the dealer has a new customer. Then he can charge the kid high prices for the coke.

For many years cocaine was not a problem in the United States. In 1914 it became against the law. Then the drug went on a long vacation. The public stopped using it because it was not safe.

**28** Cocaine was also expensive. Most people couldn't afford it at first.

When the 1980s came along, cocaine was called the "champagne of drugs." That meant that it was the best drug. It meant that cocaine was a drug for rich, trendy people. Movie stars and rock stars were using cocaine. Professional basketball, football, and baseball players were using cocaine. Rich men and women were using cocaine. It was the drug for "glamorous" people.

Popular actors, rock stars, and sports figures continue to have health problems and legal troubles caused by their abuse of cocaine, crack, and other drugs.

Scott Weiland, lead singer of the Stone Temple Pilots, checked into a drug treatment center in January 1997 after he was arrested for possession of cocaine and heroin. His drug treatment forced the popular band to cancel its concert tour and almost caused the band to break up.

Actor Robert Downey, Jr. is another young celebrity whose career has been affected by drug problems. In June 1996, Downey was arrested for driving under the influence, possession of a controlled substance (crack cocaine, powder cocaine, and black-tar heroin), and possession of a concealed weapon. In November 1996 he was sentenced to three years probation related to these charges.

Talented Dallas Cowboys wide receiver Michael Irvin also was sentenced to probation after pleading no contest in July 1996 to cocaine possession charges. He was not allowed to play in the first five games of the 1996 football season.

These stars suffered career problems and legal trouble because of their drug use. But drugs can do more than mess up your life. They can take your life. River Phoenix was a talented young actor who was nominated for an Oscar for his role in *Running on Empty*. He was popular, but like many young actors in Hollywood, he had problems with drugs. On October 31, 1993, he died after a night of partying that including taking cocaine and several other drugs. He suffered seizures and went into cardiac arrest. He was only twenty-three years old.

Many people still think that cocaine can only hurt rich people and glamorous stars. That's not true. Cocaine can kill anyone who uses it.

When police identify a crack house the dealers and buyers are
hauled off to jail.

# CHAPTER 4

# The Dangers of Crack

*S*norting cocaine up your nose is not the only way to take it. Drug dealers have invented ways to change the cocaine powder so that users can smoke it.

Crack is an extremely dangerous form of cocaine. It is made by mixing cocaine with baking soda and water. It is boiled into a paste. Then it hardens. The result is a "rock" of crack. It's called crack because of the sound it makes when smoked. It looks like a small white chip.

Freebasing is another way to smoke cocaine. In freebasing, powdered cocaine is mixed with ether (a liquid that is also used as a painkiller). The powder is mixed with other chemicals too, and a cocaine base is formed.

When it is smoked in freebase or

*32* crack form, cocaine affects the user's body faster than in powdered form. The drug goes to the user's lungs and then to his brain. It happens very fast.

Freebasing is very risky. It causes hallucinations. You see things that aren't really there. It causes paranoia. You think the world is out to get you.

Freebasing also causes health problems. It can cause a heart attack. It can make you have a stroke. Freebasing messes up your lungs, your brain, your heart, and your life.

Richard Pryor, the famous comedian, was freebasing in 1982. The ether he was using exploded. His body was badly burned. He almost died. Drug dealers invented crack in part because it is easier to make than freebase. The process of making crack is safer than freebasing. Many people who freebased in the past now use crack instead.

Crack is in a form that is ready to smoke. The dealers can sell a rock for $10 or $20 a piece. A hit of crack is cheaper than a hit of powdered cocaine. The high is much more intense. And younger people can afford it. But crack is not safe. It is a powerful and dangerous drug.

# What Is Special About Crack?

What is so special about crack? Why is it getting so much attention? There are many reasons. More and more people are becoming addicted to it. The crime rate has gone up. Thousands of crack babies are born each year. There are many more reasons. Let's look at these reasons more closely.

You know that crack is cheap. It is sold on the streets, ready to smoke. You can buy it almost everywhere. That is why crack is called the "fast food of drugs." In some cities, buying crack is as easy as getting a hamburger at McDonald's.

*34*     You also know that thousands of people are addicted to crack. They buy a lot of it. And addicts always want more. So the drug dealers need to buy more cocaine to make the crack. They buy it from drug traffickers in South America. The country of Peru grows 33 tons of coca leaves each year. The country of Bolivia grows 38 tons each year. The coca leaves are turned into cocaine. Much of this cocaine comes to the United States through drug traffickers. Then the dealers turn the cocaine into crack and sell it on the streets.

A single hit of crack costs less than a single hit of powder cocaine. A rock of crack costs between $5 and $20. Cocaine is sold in grams. A gram costs between $45 and $150. The low price of crack makes it possible for anybody to buy.

But what is the real cost? Crack smokers get high and then "crash." Users want more crack to get over the depression they feel. They have to spend another $10 or $20 to get more crack. If they buy crack ten times in a week, they've spent between $100 and $200. Powder cocaine seems to cost more than crack. But, in the end, crack costs more because the users need more of it.

Crack makes addicts faster than any other drug.

Crack began to get attention around 1985. Its low price makes it special. Almost anyone can afford a $10 piece. Crack is also special because the high is very intense. The drug is smoked in a pipe. It goes straight to the lungs and brain. People become addicted quickly. So crack became very popular. Within a few months crack was in most major cities. Now it is very easy to buy even in small cities and towns.

**36** Crack is also special because the dealers are very well organized. They have set up special houses for their customers. The houses are called "crack houses." The dealers sell crack in these houses. The users also smoke crack in these houses. It gives them a place to go and get high. They don't have to take a chance of getting caught on the street. They also don't have to do it at home. The crack houses are very handy for users.

Cocaine powder is snorted up the nose. Some of it is absorbed by the body. It takes the drug three or four minutes to reach the brain. Crack is different here too. It is smoked, as you know. But crack reaches the lungs and brain in *less than 10 seconds*. Whereas cocaine takes a few minutes, crack takes only a few seconds.

Cocaine powder will keep you high for two or three *hours*. Crack will keep you high for only five or ten *minutes*. The crack high is followed by a big low. The user becomes very depressed. The user feels sad and alone. The depression is hard to endure. The user buys another rock of crack and smokes it to forget the depression. That is how people become addicted so quickly. As soon as they crash, they want to get high again.

Because it is smoked, crack is stronger than powder cocaine. The strength of crack makes it very addictive. Crack is ten times more addictive than cocaine that is snorted. Some users say that they were hooked by the first or second hit. *Crack is the most addictive drug known to man.* That is another reason it is special compared to other drugs. That is also why it's so scary.

People can overdose on crack too. An overdose can happen at any time. It can happen a few minutes after using. It can happen an hour after using. An overdose happens when the body gets too much cocaine. You lose control of your body. You begin to have body spasms called *seizures.* You can pass out or go into a coma. If you don't get medical help, you will die.

Crack hurts everybody. It is dangerous for many reasons. Since it hit the streets, crime has gone way up. Crack houses are guarded by teenagers with guns. Street gangs get involved too.

Crack users run out of money. They steal to get money to buy more. Teenagers have started selling drugs to make money. Some also sell their bodies for sex to get money to buy more crack.

**38**    People on crack feel as if they can take on the world. They feel powerful and get angry over little things. Often they become violent. Violence is also connected to the gangs that sell the drugs and their dangerous methods of defending their territories.That is why crack is blamed for a big increase in the number of drug-related murders.

A crack house is sealed up after a raid so that it cannot go back into business.

Crack dealers can make millions of dollars. They fight over territory to get more customers. Street gangs in Los Angeles, New York, and many other major cities are fighting over crack.

*39*

Drug dealers and users are also having a war with the police. The police want the crime to end. Sixty percent of all crimes are related to drug use. If people stopped taking drugs, the crime rate would drop.

The police also blame crack for the increase in teen crime. Since crack became popular, crime has gone way up. People turn to robbery, drug dealing, or prostitution to earn money for crack. The dealers are making millions of dollars. They murder others who get in their way.

A federal government report says that the number of youths using cocaine at least monthly rose 166 percent in 1996. Crime-fighting agencies fear what will happen when these violent teens reach their twenties.

Crack can destroy many lives. Women who smoke crack during pregnancy harm their babies. These "crack babies" are born addicted to the drug. Depending on the study, researchers estimate that as many as 160,000 crack

When a parent is hooked on drugs, the children face a sad future.

babies are born each year in the United States.

Crack babies have problems with their lungs. They have problems with their heart. They need more medical attention than regular babies. Many crack babies have mental problems too. They have trouble adjusting to everyday life because of crack.

This drug doesn't care who you are. Young people and old people use crack. Rich people and poor people use crack. Black people and white people use crack. Even mothers and fathers use crack.

Child abuse and neglect have risen because of crack. Parents who use it can't think about their children. They forget to feed the kids. They spend the money on drugs instead of food. They get angry at the kids very easily, too. In New York City, the number of children in foster care has more than tripled due to the effects of crack. That doesn't mean that the parents don't love their kids. It means that crack is messing up their minds. They love the high that crack gives them. Crack addicts have no control over themselves.

## Things to Remember

Crack is smoked. It is sold on the street for a low price. Anybody can afford to buy it. All types of people smoke crack. It is ten times more powerful than powder cocaine. Anyone can overdose on crack—even first-time users.

Crime rates have risen because of crack. It makes people feel powerful and violent. People steal, cheat, lie, or sell their bodies for crack. It is the *most addictive* drug known to humans. Pregnant women and parents who use crack are destroying the lives of many children. That is what makes crack so special. That's why crack gets so much attention.

In filthy surroundings, crack addicts gather to smoke the drug in secret.

# People Who Use Crack

*F*or the last thirty years drugs have been very popular. They have a role in everyday life.  Television and music videos show the exciting, fast-paced life of drinking and drug use. Some movies show young people partying, getting drunk, and getting high, making it all look fun. For years popular music has been saying that drugs are cool.

Today, many rock and rap artists sing about drugs.  Nirvana, Alice in Chains, and Depeche Mode all sing about using heroin, while The Beastie Boys, Cypress Hill, and Snoop Doggy Dog openly promote smoking marijuana in their song lyrics. Many teens admire celebrities and are influenced by what they say and do. This may be one of the reasons for the increase in teen drug use.

44    Recent figures show that 1.5 million people in the United States use cocaine. Among young people, the rate of cocaine use is up. It has doubled for eighth-graders during the past five years.

Crack addiction *is* a big deal. Crack severely damages a person's lungs, brain, and heart. It can cause people to hallucinate, and also makes people violent. Crack use has created many more problems around the world.

One recent report says that crack is so plentiful in some cities that the same vial that was $20 a few years ago now costs $3. Powdered cocaine can still cost up to $150 for one gram. In some places, crack is more affordable and accessible than ever.

Why do people use crack? Because it's available and the high is intense. One user said the high from crack is "otherworldly." Another said, "Crack is everything you expect with powder cocaine—multiplied a zillion times. And once you feel that way, you want to do it again and again."

But crack is not glamorous. "I stole, lied, cheated, and manipulated," said one crack user of her experience. Crack users sit in filthy, smelly crackhouses to get high. They sell their abused bodies for sex to buy more crack. There's nothing glamorous or mysterious about it.

Though crack costs less than other drugs, it's not as cheap as people think. A crack high lasts only 5 or 10 minutes. The users want to get high again right away. They end up buying more, so in the end it actually costs more. The user needs more of it, more often.

Some people say that crack makes your sex life better. They may be right, at first. But repeated use of crack often causes impotence in men. That means that their penis can't get erect. Then they can't have sex at all.

Some people trade sex for crack. And the number of sexual diseases has gone up. Health workers say that sexual diseases are spreading because people are using drugs such as crack.

Every person has three basic drives. These drives are for food, water, and sex. A crack addict always needs crack. The need for the drug overpowers the basic drives for food, water, and sex. That just proves that crack will not make your sex life better. It will make you forget about food, water, and sex.

When a teenager begins to neglect the important things—even eating—he may have a drug problem.

# CHAPTER 7

# Crack and You

*P*eople on crack change their whole lives. We know that using crack leads to crime. People steal from their family and friends. Crack users lie and cheat to get money to buy it. Other things also happen.

Drug users start hanging out with other drug users. They leave their old friends behind. Crack users lose interest in school. They don't care about work except to get money. They don't care about how they look. Drug users start dressing sloppy and not washing. They don't care about being around other people.

Crack smokers destroy their body. Your brain is the control center for your entire

*47*

**48** body. When crack affects your brain, it changes the way your eyes work. Bright light starts to hurt your eyes. Objects look fuzzy. Some crack smokers see floating objects from the corners of their eyes. Some users see little rings of light around objects. These are called "snow" lights. The crack smoker may also see two of everything.

The lungs and throat are also in trouble. Crack smoking can cause a sore throat. It can also lead to an illness called bronchitis. This makes it hard to breathe.

Smoking crack makes your body weak. Many users don't get hungry. They would rather get high than eat. So they don't eat food. Then they lose weight. The body can't fight off diseases when it is weak. That is how crack smokers get sick.

Crack users start having hallucinations. They see things that aren't there. They become paranoid. They think that everyone is out to get them. Crack also messes up your heart. It makes the heart work faster. Blood pressure goes up. Your body temperature also goes up. The body becomes weak because of the drugs. So does the heart. Using crack can make you have a heart attack. Even young, healthy people have heart attacks when they use crack.

Remember that crack users also get depressed without the drug. They get moody. One minute they are happy. The next minute they are mean. Crack users begin to spend more time alone. Crack becomes the most important thing. They forget about hobbies. They don't care about school or work. Crack addicts also forget about their family and friends. They don't care about anything but getting high on crack.

Getting high makes them depressed. This depressed, lonely feeling is strong. Some crack users try to commit suicide when they experience the crash that comes after every high.

Good friends and playing sports are a big help in avoiding the dangers of drugs.